DATA

DETECTIVE

Padmaraj Nidagundi

DEDICATION

If you have ever thought to yourself, "I want to become Data Detective or I want to enhance my skills for the future data-driven job market" then this is a perfect book for you. In the book, the author comes up with some important themes: Skills need to become a data detective, Representing data to management and so on.

In the book, the author comes up with some important themes:

History Of Data Detective
Becoming A Data Detective
Data Detective Challenges And Opportunities
Data Detective In Agile Era
Skills Need To Become Data Detective
Data Detective: Data Detective Data Munging And
Finding Patterns
Data Detective: Creating Computerised Models To Extract
The Data
Data Detective: Removing Corrupted Data
Data Detective: Perform Initial Analysis To Assess The
Quality Of The Data
Data Detective: Determine The Meaning Of The Data
Data Detective: Final Analysis To Provide Additional Data
Screening
Data Detective: Representing Data To Management
Self Q&A

CONTENTS

1. HISTORY OF DATA DETECTIVE 6

2. BECOMING A DATA DETECTIVE 9

3. DATA DETECTIVE CHALLENGES AND OPPORTUNITIES 13

4. DATA DETECTIVE IN AGILE ERA 18

5. SKILLS NEED TO BECOME DATA DETECTIVE ...21

6. IOT DATA: COLLECT, PROCESS, AND ANALYZE 25

7. DATA DETECTIVE: HOW TO FIND KNOWLEDGE AND INSIGHTS IN DATA 34

8. DATA DETECTIVE: HANDING LARGE SET IOT SENSOR DATA...41

9. QUANTUM COMPUTING AND QUANTUM INFORMATION SCIENCE 47

10. QUANTUM COMPUTING FOR LARGEST OF DATA HANDLING 52

11. DATA DETECTIVE: DATA DETECTIVE DATA MUNGING AND FINDING PATTERNS 55

12. DATA DETECTIVE: CREATING COMPUTERISED MODELS TO EXTRACT THE DATA.......................59

13. DATA DETECTIVE: REMOVING CORRUPTED DATA..62

14. DATA DETECTIVE: PERFORM INITIAL ANALYSIS TO ASSESS THE QUALITY OF THE DATA 68

15. DATA DETECTIVE: DETERMINE THE MEANING OF THE DATA 75

16. DATA DETECTIVE: FINAL ANALYSIS TO PROVIDE ADDITIONAL DATA SCREENING...........78

17. DATA DETECTIVE: REPRESENTING DATA TO MANAGEMENT..81

18. DATA DETECTIVE BIG DATA AND AI/ML 85

FOLLOW ALONG THE JOURNEY 90

1. HISTORY OF DATA DETECTIVE

Data In Past:

We collected data from customers in business all the time. However, it is not always so easy to analyze what each customer bought. Data in business is sometimes not so easily understood. For example, data of businesses analyzed only by the years last year would be a huge loss because they have left us already.

Data In Present:

Today, Data is used by tens of thousands of people every day, including researchers, journalists, teachers, students—even patients with Parkinson's disease. In the modern world, we have a wide range of opportunities to collect data that comes from all around us and forms a powerful marketing tool for many companies and organizations.

Data in the 2021 century become the backbone for business. The process of turning data into valuable information is Data Detective. How did the term 'Data Detective' come to be in the first place? The phrase was in use in 2008. It is a way to describe people who are responsible for using technology tools and techniques to extract valuable information from large amounts of data. Data Detective jobs typically require advanced knowledge skills, expertise with technology, mathematics, and statistical analysis skills.

As a member of the Data team, you will work with individuals and teams across our organization to generate meaningful business answers and recommendations from the investigation of data generated by the

1. Internet of Things endpoints
2. Devices
3. Sensors
4. Biometric monitors
5. Traditional computing infrastructure
6. Next-gen fog mesh edge neural capabilities
7. Advanced artificial intelligence algorithms
8. And data streaming from the cloud… etc

Today, Data Detective jobs are rapidly changing. It continues to evolve as technology improves and the types of data being processed change. Data Detective jobs are growing rapidly in many industries worldwide. The demand for Data Detective jobs is expected to increase by 17% between now and 2030. This is much faster than average for all other occupations requiring similar skill sets.

Data Is Future:

We are rapidly expanding our services with new different types of devices and software to meet the needs of all data users who need low- or high-tech data tools for their work. We are growing our technology to meet the increasing demand for data services. The plans are to help researchers, journalists, teachers, students—even patients with Parkinson's disease. In future, you might see a war between corporates for customer data, numerous hacks aimed at stealing data, and at the same time strict security policies.

in the future data collected from different sources, new types of devices and technology help us to achieve this goal. Data Detective will be someone who can help you solve this problem.

2. BECOMING A DATA DETECTIVE

. If you know a little bit about data, but don't know how to become a professional Data Detective with skills in statistics, machine learning, and probability theory, you're not alone. Though these are the three most common skillsets for professionals to have in the field of data analytics, there are plenty of other skills needed to be considered an expert.

Figure for skills need to become a data detective

This chapter will cover some of those types of skills that would make you stand out as an analyst who can really dive into their work and find clear results quickly.

What are the Skills Needed to Become a Data Detective?

1. Data Processing

Excel, SAS, SPSS Getting data from one place to another is the first hurdle of the job, so being able to use these programs is important. If you have more significant knowledge of these programs or have more study time under your belt, having more complex software under your belt will give you an advantage over others.

2. Data Visualization & Communication

3. Data Analysis

SPSS, SAS, Matlab, Mathematica A set of data analysis programs such as these is a must if you want to be a Data Detective. These programs allow you to complete complex calculations and techniques with ease. If you don't have any experience with these kinds of programs, they can be tough to learn on your own.

4. Data Mining

La- La- LAAAMM! One of the most commonly asked questions is, "how do you get data to be of more significant value for your company?" Data mining is the answer. The process of taking your massive amounts of data and finding where different sets of data are grouped or overlap together.

5. Data Science

The last and final step in becoming a data scientist is to put all the pieces together and understand how they work together in a cohesive way. This can be the hardest, but the most rewarding step in your journey.

6. Programming

Python, R Programming is another skill that is not needed for everyone, but certainly helps when it comes to furthering your career as a Data Detective rather than having to rely solely on manual calculations.

7. Data Collection

Different digital devices, different data sources such as IoT, Biometrics, social media, etc.

8. Data Analysis

Analytics tools such as SQL, Elasticsearch, NoSQL databases, etc.

9. Data Science Practice

Data science projects to apply your newly acquired skills to further your career as a data scientist or analytics professional. Projects could be based on applications you've built for different work environments or things that help you understand the field of data science more fully.

10. Data Related Laws:

For example, GDPR, HIPAA, etc. and Law according to each country where your use base located.

As we can see from the list, we put together there are plenty of skills and steps needed to become a Data Detective. Being able to find all these what you need to become a Data Detective is only half the battle. You will need to work hard and dedicate yourself fully to your new profession if you want to reach the top levels of the field.

3. DATA DETECTIVE CHALLENGES AND OPPORTUNITIES

In the future data is generated by the "N" number of sources from a user point of view or business point of view. such as:

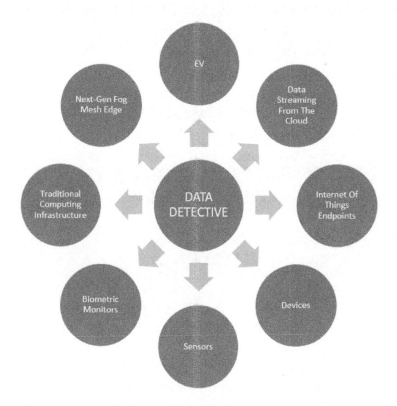

Figure for future data is generated by the "N" number of sources.

- Internet Of Things Endpoints
- Devices

- Sensors
- Biometric Monitors
- Traditional Computing Infrastructure
- Next-Gen Fog Mesh Edge Neural Capabilities
- Advanced Artificial Intelligence Algorithms
- EV - Electric Cars, Scooters Or Any Vehicles
- Data Streaming From The Cloud...Etc.

When data was started generated from various sources. Currently, much of the data we collect from these areas go unexamined, but this will change.

As the data becomes available, business leaders, the government and researchers are scrambling to figure out how to use it to their advantage. With all that data, there is value in it for everyone. That is why competition will increase in this space. The unique skill set needed to analyze these various kinds of data will be in high demand.

CHALLENGES

The Challenges For This Area Will Be:

Gathering all the data, identifying the relevant information and understanding its applications.

Analyzing the data and getting an understanding of what is important.

Sampling and benchmarking to find patterns. Processing and sorting out data with multiple sources such as sensor data, logs, network activity and more. This activity will also focus on developing algorithms that can combine these various sources of data into a meaningful whole.

The Challenges For This Area Will Be:

IoT sensors and the cloud as the generating source of data, as well as the next generation fog (edge) machine learning capabilities. There is currently a lot of work in a traditional computing infrastructure to take advantage of these various SaaS and IaaS data streaming technologies. However, much of what we now do today does not scale to support IoT and edge workloads and will require new technologies.

Data will need to be accessible, secure, flexible and able to be analyzed at any level. For example, local data analysis for an IoT endpoint device being able to communicate with backend data storage servers, which then communicate with cloud-based artificial intelligence algorithms that can analyze the data and apply it back to the device for localized real-time changes.

Local data processing at the edge will allow for real-time decisions.

OPPORTUNITIES

The Opportunities For This Area Will Be

We will need to create hybrid solutions where we combine traditional and next-gen logic and data capabilities. These hybrid solutions will be able to process and analyze data for multiple sources. They will also be able to handle the IoT edge workloads while providing security, scalability and flexibility. This combination of technologies should allow us to get the most out of our IoT investments while minimizing the workload on our traditional computing infrastructure.

This space will also include the ability to automatically generate algorithms for complex data analysis. That means you can take data from any source, apply it to an algorithm and have the results returned in real-time. This will allow you to determine if there are any problems in your systems, issues with your processes or if there are any patterns in your data that can be used for predictive analytics.

There are already a number of companies out there working on these technologies, but the need for solutions is still large. What differentiates our solution is the ability to combine multiple data sources, tools and applications into a cohesive system so people can clearly see what they are looking at, understand it and then be able to take real-time actions based on that information.

The roadmap to implement these solutions will start with understanding the processes that are currently running in the current systems. This includes looking at all the I/O devices, how they are configured. Identifying which data needs to be collected by which endpoint. Understanding what data is needed in the current system and how it will be stored in the future.

Once you have this information, you can begin to design your hybrid systems. The hybrid solutions will combine the various technologies needed to support IoT edge, fog and

AI processing. These systems may include advanced artificial intelligence algorithms that will use a combination of log data, sensor data, traditional computing infrastructure and the cloud. You can then begin to think about where the data will be stored. Will it reside on your local storage systems, in the cloud or a combination of both?

The hybrid approach should provide a versatile environment that will help maximize the performance of your IoT edge devices while giving you the capabilities of traditional computing infrastructure and cloud-based technologies. The applications for this space will also be a hybrid solution that combines a traditional user interface along with an advanced artificial intelligence algorithm.

This area will take a lot of time and effort to implement, but it will be worth it. The impact on your current business processes and workflows will be huge, especially if you provide an easy-to-use interface that allows anyone to analyze data from any source locally or in the cloud.

There are a lot of companies battling for dominance in this space, but I believe we have a significant differentiator that should position us well as we move forward.

4. DATA DETECTIVE IN AGILE ERA

In the future data is generated by the "N" number of sources from which companies need to draw. Because data is a primary type of input for a business, the importance of a Data Detective has increased significantly even as other roles have been left behind, reducing the overall amount of people doing these jobs. Data analytics jobs require different skills from other jobs. It requires strong mathematical abilities, and it also requires analytical thinking and problem-solving skills.

Technical Part

As we see the requirement for data is growing and we can see more and more sources for the data in future.

Data Detective is in a critical role in preparing and analyzing big data in real-time. The problem in preparing and analyzing big data is that, when there are a huge amount of unstructured data stored in the databases, it is impossible to perform analysis by using current tools like SQL or Tableau (because of its complexity).

One of the solutions that can be used to solve the above problem is to use unstructured data stored in databases because unstructured data stored in databases provides a structured way of retrieving the data.

To utilize unstructured data stored in databases, it should be analyzed by using certain tools like Apache Spark to perform analysis on it. Using Apache Spark for this purpose can help us improve productivity, so it can be said that Apache Spark is an alternative solution for Hadoop Map Reduce.

After analyzing the data by using Apache Spark, we can export the results of the analysis in a structured form. For this purpose, we can use a data warehouse to store and archive the results of the analysis in a structured form. Then it can be used in other tools such as Tableau when necessary.

In summary, when handling big data which is stored in databases from one point of view, using tools like SQL or Tableau does not provide productivity because it is difficult to use them easily when there are huge amounts of data.

Data Law And Law Enforcement Knowledge

IF you want to become successful in this area you need also data law and law enforcement knowledge. Remember we are dealing here with the "N" number of data sources. In this situation, we might encounter different laws according to

1) Device which producing the data
2) Data source
3) Government or private company data policy
4) Data Encryption
5) Data Classification

Although, different data management methods are employed by different companies for these 3 categories of data.

If you want to become successful in this area, you should have a broad knowledge about the below.

1) Data Process
2) Data Management Method
3) Data Portability etc.

As an expert, this area you need technical as well as different data law knowledge. Data law and law enforcement knowledge is your unique selling point.

.

5. SKILLS NEED TO BECOME DATA DETECTIVE

Investigating data is often hazardous to your career, no matter how big the stakes. Not only is the investigator's every move under intense scrutiny, but they are also susceptible to getting boxed in by their own biases. The key to success in this niche is learning how to integrate with the people you are trying to help and understanding their perspective. Data detective skills do not come naturally; they require patience, persistence, and empathy.

Figure core skill need for data detective job

Examine data - first step is to identify and examine existent data sets generated from multiple (hardware and software) sources (e.g., home environmental sensors, organization finance function spreadsheets, etc.).

Information literacy - Identify and access relevant information through an understanding of the information landscape (e.g., taxonomy or ontology) and by using effective search strategies.

Analyze data - Apply a variety of statistical, mathematical, and other analytic techniques to one or more datasets (e.g., identify trends; detect anomalies; cluster data; display information; etc.).

Find new sources of data - Uncover new data sources that are not yet being leveraged for further investigation (e.g., smart city car parking data, office needed products and supplies rates, etc.).

Present findings - to be able to present findings in both verbal (talk) and visual (displayed-hardcopy) formats. Identifying the needs of the business to be able to find relevant information within their field. Having key insight to look at information in a different way.

Ask questions of data - "What are the dominant patterns in this data?" - "What is the current state?" - "What could change in the future?" Learn what data are collected for, where collected from, what sensors are used for, how it is collected.

I Ask questions of people - "What are you trying to solve?" - "How are you defining success?" - "Which data is useful to you right now?"

Work data sources - What is the data you are already collecting? Who collects it, where it is collected, how it is collected? What are the data elements you have in your systems? What data does your business use to make business decisions?

Triangulate different data sources - Look for a more complete view of the business through cross referencing data across multiple systems, data stores, and data types. - Combine machine/device/environmental data with human language data from surveys, questionnaires, interviews.

Connect to real people - Find out what people are already doing to measure their success.

Write reports and present findings - Create a narrative that helps people understand what's going on.

Present findings - Visualize the big picture i.e. an environment map, display data in different way, create a mind map of findings, create a report to give to management.

Keep update yourself on data science trends - Following data science trends helps in staying current on new developments.

- Set goals - Set specific goals for improvement to your skills.
- Take actions - Identify specific, achievable actions that will help you improve.
- Discuss results with others - Share your findings with colleagues and/or management to get feedbacks on what you are doing well and where you need to improve.
- Contribute to the broader community.

Data detective skills do not come naturally; they need to be developed, practiced, and polished. Knowledge won't suddenly appear when you need it most. It requires preparation, preparation, and more preparation. Before the big event, spend time gathering data on your planned interrogation sites.

Data detective skills allow you to apply methodical investigative techniques that you use every day in your business to your client's big data problem.

6. IOT DATA: COLLECT, PROCESS, AND ANALYZE

Every day, we are surrounded by sensors that detect, measure, and send data in some form. Devices and technology connected over the Internet of Things IoT can monitor and measure data in real time.

The process for collecting these data is as diverse as the types of sensors themselves. For example, some IoT devices send data to a cloud provider that is then used by the sensor's manufacturer to improve the product. These data points may beacon, motion sensors, cameras, and other types of sensors.

When there is a new IoT device deployed in your home or office space, it can often require professional assistance to become fully operational and configured for data collection. For many of these devices and technology companies who create them, security and privacy protection is an important objective.

Sensors collect various types of data, including personal identifiable information PII. Data are collected from IoT consumer devices, such as security systems, smart appliances, smart TVs, wearable health meters, or other devices that you may have in your home or office space. This data may be stored on these local devices.

By implementing an IoT device through a service provider enabled by the company creating the technology, consumers can receive IoT solutions with over-the-air updates and maintenance support. In this scenario, data is collected from multiple IoT devices and stored in the cloud. In some cases, data may be collected from a sensor and stored directly in the cloud.

Some people believe that by collecting their data in a central repository, they can take advantage of analytics to gain deeper insights into how their daily activities affect their personal health and well-being. The raw data in a central repository can also be analyzed in real time.

Using the right tools and technologies combined with IoT data, companies can offer services to develop predictive maintenance, improve energy efficiency, and help reduce waste and pollution. The value of IoT data depends on how it is used by the business and what analytics can be performed around that data.

IoT Data: How To Collect, Process, And Analyze

Various types of sensors can collect data from your home or office environment. These sensors gather information such as temperature, air quality, motion detection, traffic patterns. Sensors can often be used to manage this data and make it useful and productive. For example, a security system may be set up to automatically call or email you if there is movement in your yard or driveway.

Different types of sensors collect different types of data. Look at the chart on the right for a list of some common IoT sensors and what data they are typically good for.

As mentioned previously, you have set up your smart thermostat, so it turns itself down before you leave for work each morning.

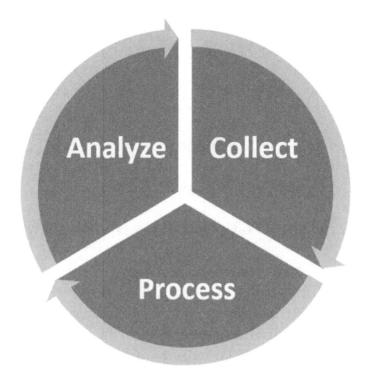

Figure for IoT "DATA" overview

Collecting IoT Data

Automation data - Data are sent to a central location, are stored in the cloud, and are processed by computers. Data are sent to a central location, are stored in the cloud, and are processed by computers.

Telemetry data - Data is transmitted over Ethernet or Wi-Fi. The data is stored on the home or office environment or on a central server. Data is transmitted over Ethernet or Wi-Fi. The data is stored on the home or office environment or on a central server.

Status data - Data is sent to a central location, is stored in the cloud, and used in real time. Data is sent to a central location, is stored in the cloud, and used in real time.

Analytics data - Data are measured using sensors and are processed by computers. The data can be analyzed in real time or processed over a period of time. This data can be used to develop modeling tools or algorithms for IoT use.

Location data - (Indoor vs outdoor data) Data is collected from GPS systems as it is transmitted over a wireless network. A smartphone can collect its location as it is sent to a cloud server.

Sensors are often used together in an IoT system. For example, in your home or business, you may have motion detectors that are linked to the alarm system in the same room. But you also have motion detectors near windows, doors, and other areas of the building. In addition, you may have a security camera in the office that is linked to a CCTV system in the same room.

In all these cases, motion data from multiple sources can be seen on a single screen. An IoT system can enable you to create a visualization of motion data so it can be acted upon in real time.

Processing IoT Data

Determining the right database for IoT data collection and analytics requires careful consideration. You need to consider the cost of setting up a database, how much data will be collected, and how much that data is worth in terms of the value it offers to a business, a government agency, a non-profit organization or any other entity. Private data are protected within the organization by encryption, password protection, firewalls, and access control methods. These security methods can keep IoT data secure, but some are also useful for consumer devices. Some consumer devices can be put into a sleep mode to protect them from monitoring outside of an organization's network. This process is called personalization.

The best strategy is often for organizations to own their own IoT data collection, processing and analytics software.

IoT Data Analytics

In the example above, a driver might be able to use their car to find the fastest route to an event they are attending at a venue. The driver may also want to know what is happening in the venue before they get there. Their car might display information about an artist who is performing, or it could provide information about any events related to that performer. This data can help the driver decide if they care about visiting that venue at all.

In recent years, there has been a lot of hype around smart cities. One example of the "smart city" trend is the use of smart parking meters. Data collected from parking meters can help cities and businesses better understand parking patterns and even which areas to focus their efforts on. Smart Parking helps cities and businesses understand and optimize their parking experience and services, making data collection more efficient and cost-effective for consumers as well as for the organization collecting the data.

Prescriptive analytics - Provides insight into likely future events through historical data analysis. Predictive analytics - Gives probable future events based on historical data analysis. Descriptive analytics - Shows what happened in the past. Diagnostic analytics - Helps you make better decisions based on more detailed analysis of data.

The value of IoT data

IoT is an information system that connects objects or devices with one another or to databases that store the data gathered by these devices. This combination of physical things, software, and networking technologies allows them to connect and exchange information with one another seamlessly. The convergence of these three things creates digital products that are more efficient, flexible, and intelligent.

The value of IoT data is immense, but many organizations are still struggling to understand where the market is headed and how to use the data that is now being generated daily.

IoT data collection, processing and analytics software offer greater value to organizations by working with their own existing systems.

Predictive Analytics - Makes predictions about future events, trends, and developments based on past data. Predictive analytics are based on historical data. It works by applying statistical calculations to the observed data in order to predict what will happen in the future. For example, a predictive model can be used to predict how long an item will take to arrive at a warehouse based on historical data of the carrier's delivery time.

Telemetry Data - Data is transmitted over Ethernet or Wi-Fi. The data is stored locally on the home or office environment or elsewhere on the network, on a central server. Status data - Data is sent to a central location, is stored in the cloud, and used in real time.

Analytics Data - Data are measured using sensors and are processed by computers. The data can be analyzed in real time or processed over a period of time. This data can be used to develop modeling tools or algorithms for IoT use.

Descriptive analytics - Gathers data that is analyzed to describe what happened in the past . It can be used to measure current trends and improve the efficiency of an organization. For example, an analyst may want to understand how current trends are impacting sales of a specific product line or service.

The business benefits from being able to tailor its offerings for each customer. The convergence of these three things creates digital products that are more efficient, flexible, and intelligent.

Spatial analytics - Determines patterns based on data from location sensors. The patterns can be analyzed to predict future trends and also to define how an organization can best serve a specific market in the future.

Big data is a term that refers to datasets that are so large they exceed the processing capacity of commonly available software tools. It is often used synonymously with "deep learning," "machine learning," and "artificial intelligence. Transactive analytics - A combination of data analytics and transactive computing. This term refers to the process of analyzing data in real time for business decisions on the job. It is often used to describe the use of location-based applications by smart phones, such as using phone GPS to understand how customers are traveling and adjusting prices accordingly.

Streaming analytics - Determines patterns or trends in real time by processing data continuously. It takes advantage of data mining, artificial intelligence, machine learning, and advanced analytics to make decisions about key business issues. The company must determine if its data resources are adequate. The size of the data resource may represent a hard limit to the amount of decision-making possible.

Time series analytics - A combination of time series and data mining. This term is used to describe a type of data mining that focuses on problems where a set of observations follows a common pattern across time, such as the motion of stars, stock prices, or wages. Temporal analytics - Provides insight into past events through historical data analysis. It uses data from different time periods to gain insights into how change occurs over time. For example, if an organization has a set of customer data that is relatively consistent across time, it may be able to use temporal analytics to understand how customers behave across different time periods and what changes can be predicted for each customer.

Institutional analytics - Refers to the use of big data analytics by teams within an organization. In the past, businesses used internal systems for data analysis and reporting within their own organizations. These systems were not designed for information sharing or for collaboration among employees.

Cognitive analytics - Provides insights into past events via historical data analysis. It uses data from different time periods to gain insights into how change occurs over time. For example, an organization with customer data that is relatively consistent across time may be able to use cognitive analytics to understand how customers behave across different time periods and what changes can be predicted for each customer.

7. DATA DETECTIVE: HOW TO FIND KNOWLEDGE AND INSIGHTS IN DATA

You can't always capture all the knowledge and insights in data using your naked eyes. That's why there are powerful tools that help you to organize, visualize, and discover connections that would have been invisible otherwise. It doesn't matter what type of data you have or how big it is, because there are popular tools for every step of the data analytics process.

There are a lot of Data Detective tools but generally, they can be divided into two groups:

1. Visualization tools – help you to organize and visualize your data on a spreadsheet. They allow you to create basic charts and plots, for example, pie charts or bar diagrams. Good knowledge of basic statistics is required to use this type of tool effectively as there is no automation in methods or processes.

2. Automated tools – are used to analyze large amounts of data. They require little knowledge of statistics, but sometimes it's necessary to understand how certain algorithms work. These tools are very popular because they generate insights automatically based on the data and their usage is simpler than that of visualizations.

No matter which type of tool you choose, there are four

main aspects you should keep in mind:

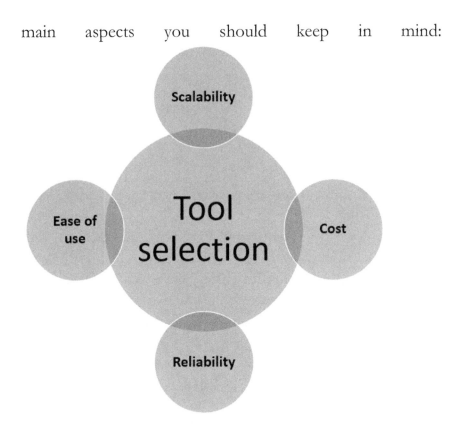

Figure for tool selection

1. Scalability – an important feature that depends on how much data you have and the time you need for analysis.

2. Ease of use – it depends on how easy you can use the tool. It can be complicated, but if it's simple, you can save time doing the analysis.

3. Cost – sometimes design and functionality are more important than price. When cost is high, you should try to find the option that suits your needs better. For example, if there are several similar tools on the market, maybe there is a cheaper one to try (for example this Excel alternative).

4. Reliability – for Data Detective you can't risk making a mistake that might be expensive in the long run. Choose a tool that you think will be reliable and get quality results.

How To Get Started With Data Detective?

1. If you want to get started with Data Detective, start with analyzing small sets of data. This way, you won't feel overwhelmed and will get more confidence in using different tools and processes.

2. It's not necessary to understand how everything works, but it is important to get the most out of the tool. For example, if you decide to use Excel, get familiar with basic statistics and get a cheat sheet of formulas. Look for an online course about basic Excel functions and learn them well.

3. There are a lot of webinars and YouTube videos that explain different aspects of Data Detective. It's worth spending some time on watching them and learning all the principles of processing and analyzing data.

4. You can also find a mentor who will help you to analyze your data and avoid mistakes in the future.

5. Data Detective can be a long process, but don't get frustrated if you don't get the results, you expected the first time you try a tool or a process. It takes time to become a master's in data Detective, but practice makes perfect.

6. It is a good idea to start a chapter and share all results

you get with Data Detective. This way, you can get feedback from other professionals and share your knowledge.

What Tools To Use For Data Detective Iot And Machine Learning?

Tools for IoT and machine learning don't differ much from the tools described above, except one: before you can make a decision on a tool, you need to know what exactly you want to do.

For example, if you want to analyze your sensor data, make sure it is uploaded to a cloud-based platform. Every sensor has its own information and you will need a tool that will help you to use that information as well as possible. The goal should be simple – getting useful insights from the data. The more you know the sensor technology, the easier it will be for you to choose the right tool.

For example, if you want to use machine learning for prediction, use tools that are able to perform this task. For instance, there are a lot of tools that help you create algorithms for prediction with relatively modest data sets. If you want to design a model for predictive analytics with scikit-learn in Python, check out this tutorial. There are a lot of resources to learn both the language and the framework.

The most important factor that may influence your choice is a price. Often, cheaper options have fewer features and, as a result, you may have to change some things in your Data Detective to get desired results. If you want to learn more about any particular tool or process, check out an online tutorial or look at examples of work published by others. You may also ask questions in forums on Reddit or Twitter.

Finally, if you feel that you are stuck or don't know how to move forward, find a mentor who will help you not only to analyze data but also understand the principles of working with data in general.

TOP TEN TIPS ON HOW TO ANALYZE DATA

1. Don't depend on a tool, learn how it works and what you can do with it so that your decision is based on experience and rational thinking.

2. Learn the basics of processing Data Detective, statistics and programming in Python.

3. Use data visualization tools to give you an overview of your data and put it into perspective. As a result, you will have a good understanding of your data and know which information is important for further processing.

4. Never rely on just one tool – always look for another tool that will help you to get results with less or more time spent on it or with less or more money spent on it.

5. Try to find the most advanced tool for Data Detective and not an alternative with one or two differences. It's better to know how a certain tool is able to do something and need less time and money than an alternative that doesn't do anything but has some unique functions that you might want to use in the future – or just don't have

time for.

6. Read more on what you are going to do, but don't just look at the steps that have to be done for a certain task. Instead, take a look at the algorithm and learn what data is taken into account and how conclusions are drawn.

7. It is a good idea to use multiple tools for gathering data from different sources, from sensors to databases or cloud-based systems.

8. Don't waste time on complex steps or complex procedures. Instead, simplify them by using batch processes or algorithms that are already well-known.

9. When you learn the principles of data processing with scikit-learn in Python, try to apply them to your dataset with the same dataset and see if they work.

10. Practice and focus on fewer things at a time. This will help you to control the amount of data and other resources that you need to spend.

DIY: How To Prepare Sensor Data For Analysis?

Finally, don't forget about your own sensors — whether they are from your smartphone or from an industrial device. They also have machine-readable information that can help you make even more sense out of your data set, whether it is from a sensor or from an industrial device.

We Suggest That You Learn How To Prepare Data For Analysis. Here Are Some Tips On How To Do It.

1. Take time to make the sensor data machine-readable if it isn't already. This will help your Data Detective process be simpler and more effective.

2. Make sure your data is well-organized and can be easily accessed by other tools or algorithms that you find useful in processing Data Detective.

3. Check if your processing software is compatible with sensor data and can work with it.

4. Make sure you choose the tools and processes that will help you get the most value out of your sensor data and make your work more effective and efficient.

5. If possible, use open-source tools to upload data to the cloud or any other place that's accessible for analysis.

6. Instead of using publicly available data sets, look for your own data that you can use in some way or another.

Conclusion: Above steps to make sense out of the sensor and other environmental data and how to analyze them efficiently and effectively.

So, we hope that we've given you a good foundation for your IoT projects with sensors, robots, factories, and other devices. In this article, we have discussed the basic concepts of IoT and machine learning, as well as the tools they can be analyzed with.

8. DATA DETECTIVE: HANDING LARGE SET IOT SENSOR DATA

Today, we see and hear of so many buzzwords and phrases in the realm of technology: Big Data, IoT sensor data, machine learning — but what does all this mean? Where did these phrases come from and what do they represent? These topics can be overwhelming for some people.

Big Data is the latest buzzword in the IT industry, with good reasons behind it being all over the Internet. This new term has become so popular, that there are even groups of people who have created an entire subculture around this trend. Big data is currently used to describe any kind of data set — be it large, diverse and mainly unstructured — which requires massive amounts of computational processing power and storage space to store and analyze.

IoT sensor data: a subset of Big Data

One very common subset of big data is IoT sensor data. These are collected from a large number of sensors that measure almost anything, from traffic to the environment, building systems to manufacturing machinery. Currently, there are a lot of companies that try to use these stored data as efficiently as possible. A high-level goal for these companies is to make big-data analytics more accessible and apply it in any possible way.

Smartphone's sensors are one of the most popular types of IoT sensor data, with their applications ranging from monitoring traffic, temperature, air quality to the behavior of people. However, this is not the only type of sensor data. These days, we can find out more about everything around us; be it traffic on highways or trees on street corners. Often these are miniaturized sensors that monitor things like light levels, water levels in tanks and trash bins or even whether there is someone sleeping on a park bench. Not only industrial machinery and industrial equipment, but also many everyday objects on which we rely on a daily basis, can be monitored by sensors.

Google Glasses from the devices of Sergey Brin at their first display of the device in 2012.
In this article, we will discuss three different types of sensor data that are collected from industrial equipment and industrial machinery. We'll talk about our experience with these data as well as explore some of the potential applications of these data.

We have a lot of experience with this kind of sensor data. Dataloggers are a special type of IoT sensor data that measure and store data from their environment, namely the temperature, pressure and humidity at a certain time. For example, you can use these dataloggers for measuring the temperature in chemical tanks or even the temperature of spare parts in a car factory. In this article we will look at three different real-life situations where we used datalogger data to improve our products.

Handing Large Set Iot Sensor Data

In this chapter, we will discuss strategies for handling large sets of sensor data. In particular, we will show how to do batch processing on a single computer using Apache Spark and Apache Flink.

Processing big data in a few gigabytes of memory is getting more common with the increased availability of very large sensors. Hence, our goal is to find a solution for converting raw sensor readings into meaningful values at what is called real-time speed or near real-time speed. This may be the case for example if you want to estimate how many customers are currently in your store.

As mentioned above, Apache Spark and Apache Flink are perfect solutions for this task because they provide strong batch processing while providing up-to-date data access to real-time or near real-time applications. Many companies are running production workloads with Spark and Flink, because the two clusters reduce costs, improve performance, and scale-out easily, thus making them well suited for large sensor data sets.

Batch Processing with Apache Spark

In particular, Apache Spark makes batch processing very easy. It supports a wide variety of file formats, including text files, sequence files, and other structured and semi-structured files. In addition to Spark's own file format (parquet), Spark also supports many general-purpose file formats such as Avro or JSON.

Spark can run on a variety of cluster managers such as YARN or Mesos. If you are running on YARN, Spark can leverage the distributed file system provided by the YARN resource manager.[1]

Apache Spark is very fast when it comes to reading data from files, but when processing large data sets in memory, it may be slow. Therefore, in this chapter we will focus on how to process big data sets in memory instead of in files.

To demonstrate the use of batch processing in Spark, we will use two simple examples: sampling stock prices and counting emails.

Example 1: Stock Price Sampling
Let us assume we have a live ticker feed with stocks in the US that we would like to sample. We could download and parse the feed and store that in a text file in order to be able to process it in a batch. However, we will assume for this example that we already have a procedure to receive data from Yahoo!, one of the largest stock prices feeds available, which is called getOpenFTS() . This function receives a list of symbols, which are the tickers to be sampled, and writes the input stream to an array in memory.

To be able to process this data in batch, we will use Spark Streaming. This is possible because Spark has built-in support for streaming files using Spark sources. It is important to note that at present, there is no support for real-time or near real-time for Spark Streaming (see the end of this chapter for more information). Spark Streaming is implemented in Java and Scala and, in addition to the Java API, there is also a Scala API for Spark Streaming. We will use the Scala API to demonstrate its use here.

First, we need to turn the incoming stream into a DStream. This allows us to process this data in batch using Spark's parallelism. Spark can distribute data across many different threads for parallel processing using shared variables. DStreams are created from action over an input. To use Spark Streaming, we need to create a StreamingContext and pass it to the StreamingContext.builder :

```scala
package com.daml.platform.sandbox.banner

import java.io.PrintStream

import scala.io.Source

object Banner {
  def show(out: PrintStream): Unit = {
    val resourceName = "banner.txt"
    if (getClass.getClassLoader.getResource(resourceName) != null)
      out.println(
        Source
          .fromResource(resourceName)
          .getLines
          .mkString("\n"))
    else
      out.println("Banner resource missing from classpath.")
  }
}
```

Here, we are creating a Spark Streaming context that will allow us to feed data into inputDStream , which is a DStream in our case. This is the DStream that contains the raw data in memory. To make sure that data can be fed at any time, we added Seconds (10) , which is the amount of time in seconds between two samples of data. The Spark

Streaming context will close the socket after the timeout.

Now that we have our DStream, we can process it using all of Spark's available transformations. For example, to sample the data every five minutes, we can divide each line by 5 seconds and then collect 100 lines at a time into an array that contains five batches over 100 seconds.

This will read the text file stock-tickers.txt, which contains stock tickers, saves its lines as an array of strings, divides each line by 5 seconds, and transforms each array into one array of five samples at a time. The output is an array of 100 batches over 10 seconds that contain the stocks that were sampled in that batch for this interval.

What we need to consider before handing in a large set of IoT sensor data: Data is coming in right now, is it really available at no additional cost? If so, why not use it to optimize your robots, sensors, and other devices?

Data is not free. To make IoT work for you, you need to look at costs. For example, if data is coming in now, it may be cheaper to just take it now. However, to be cost-efficient in the long term, you will want to batch the data and only process the data when there is a large amount of data available or when batch processing provides better efficiencies than real-time analyzers.

By using Spark Streaming's transformation API you can modify the incoming data set to your liking. This also allows you to do something like sampling the data by time or sampling the data by space (location). This is useful when you want to improve efficiency through parallelization.

9. QUANTUM COMPUTING AND QUANTUM INFORMATION SCIENCE

The human brain is a typically recognized biological quantum computer, and the eye is also considered to be a photonic quantum computer.

What Is Quantum Computing?

· The fundamental unit of computation in classical computers is the bit.

· The fundamental unit of computation in quantum computers are qubits.

· A qubit can exist in all states at once, but must collapse into one state upon measurement. This ability to store many bits within one physical object enables more powerful processing than that available with classical computing alone.

What Are the Benefits of Quantum Computing?

· Quantum computing has the benefit of being able to

solve otherwise unsolvable problems, such as factoring very large numbers, searching databases and modeling physical systems. The computational power of quantum computers will help enterprises in a variety of fields from the financial sector to the academic sector.

What Are Some Examples of Quantum Computing Use Cases?

· In 2017, Dr. Stephen Hawking and his colleagues at the University of Cambridge published a paper in Nature describing an experiment(1) in which quantum computation led to the prediction of three possible states for a particle. This is the first time that quantum computing enabled scientists to make an observation not previously possible.

· The Google Quantum AI Lab has recently announced its goal to build a 'universal' computer that can solve problems that currently stump classical computers. Quantum computing will allow for this, because it can hack through complex algorithms rather than brute-force trying all combinations of inputs.

· Another quantum computing use case is in improving the accuracy of weather forecasting models. A recent breakthrough in this field enabled scientists to improve the accuracy of weather forecasts by up to 40 percent.

· IBM has built a prototype quantum computer that can potentially outperform conventional computers, but hasn't yet turned it into many useful applications.

What Are the Challenges Faced by Quantum Computing?

· Many of the early attempts at building a commercialized quantum computer have met with difficulty. For example, at the end of 2016, Google's Quantum AI Lab disbanded(2) after a team of quantum physicists led by Dr. Luk Vandenburg found that they were unable to build a device that could solve certain problems.

· However, the technology is becoming more accessible with each passing year. Increasingly powerful quantum computers are being built – and a number of these devices are now available for purchase from companies such as Lockheed Martin and D-Wave Systems.

Who Is Leading Quantum Computing Development?

· The best-known company developing a commercial quantum computer is D-Wave Systems.
· D-Wave Systems has been developing quantum computers for nearly 20 years. Since 2000, the company has sold more than 1000 devices worldwide and claims that it has processed 2 million qubits.

What Has Been Researched by Quantum Computing?

In 2016 the European Space Agency conducted a study into what impact quantum computing could have on future space travel(3). The study concluded that the ability of a quantum computer to solve certain mathematical problems could make future space travel more efficient and accurate.

How Do Scientists Access Quantum Computing Resources?

There are few resources available to those interested in learning how to become experts in quantum computing. The most accessible resources for those interested in becoming experts in quantum computing include:

· National Instruments(4) provides information on how to build and program a quantum computer.

· Dr. Matt Visser(5) has been quoted as saying that "You can implement quantum computing in a way that makes it look very much like a regular computer.", and provides a tutorial on how to access a quantum computer online.

Quantum information science is the interdisciplinary study of quantum computing, quantum information theory, computation and information. The research field includes quantum chemistry, molecular electronics, cryptography and especially the applications of these technologies for areas such as encryption, distributed computing and coding theory. Quantum information science was pioneered by Richard Feynman.

Digital integrated circuits (ICs) are built with transistors operated at room temperature on all their active elements to save current consumption. The main advantage of transistors is that, unlike other technologies such as laser diodes and LEDs, they require only a small amount of power to operate. The low-power consumption arises from the fact that the current passing through the transistor is negligible.

Transistors are generally used as switches used to control currents and voltages. While there has been no fundamental change in the design of these devices for over fifty years, their evolution has been driven by technological considerations and price/performance goals.

Over time, transistors migrated from the point-contact to the planar structure. At first, a current-carrying path was drawn on a gas-filled metal plate on which a voltage pulse would be applied to switch the current on and off. As transistors became smaller, this technology proved problematic as there was insufficient space for contacts. In 1962, Leo Esaki discovered that it is possible to place a thin layer of semiconductor between two fine wires for direct connection rather than using bulky metal electrodes.

10. QUANTUM COMPUTING FOR LARGEST OF DATA HANDLING

The function of a computer may be to do computational operations, but they are limited by the speed at which they can perform calculations. To solve this problem, scientists have invented quantum computers. These computers are built on the principle of quantum mechanics and use an atom-like principle called superposition to store information in multiple states. However, the basic principles of quantum computers like superposition are not properly understood by experts today.

Quantum computing is here to stay. The latest review article on these subject states that the only limits to quantum computing are not scientific or technological but related to economic considerations. Much progress has been made in this field over the last 2 decades. Already several companies are marketing quantum computers, but these are compact devices for limited applications. The number of qubits is in the order of 10 to 12 for current-generation devices.

Nuclear magnetic resonance techniques are used in this

study 8,9 to perform quantum mechanical simulations. NMR technology allows very high-quality experimental data to be obtained. These data are used in this study to arrive at a better understanding of the foundations of quantum computing. These processes are also being carried out on supercomputers using different algorithms.

Quantum Computer For Data detective

Quantum computers are superior to conventional computers in terms of computational speed, memory and the amount of data that can be stored. Quantum computers will be able to perform calculations on a vast amount of data with high accuracy, which is not possible with the conventional approach. This is true for most research fields, but especially so for data analysis which deals with huge amounts of data and performs multidimensional computations and tests difficult to solve by conventional computers.

Quantum computing is much faster than traditional computers for handling huge amounts of data. Quantum computers can handle much more data at much faster speeds than which conventional computers are used today. This is because the information stored in quantum bits called qubits can be manipulated in any state at the same time. The binary bits conventionally used in computers are limited to conducting one operation at a time, but qubits are capable of conducting two or more operations simultaneously.

The two most famous decoherence models are Deutsch et al. 9,10 and Del Zanna 13,14. The first model is one of the most debated quantum computing techniques in the literature. This model states that there are three types of decoherence namely, single-shot decoherence (SSD), dephasing (where both measurement and qubit state collapse) and shared memory (or mutual information worse than the sum of the individual copies). The shared memory decoherence needs more steps to lead to a full collapse of qubit measurement.

The second model focuses on the idea that quantum computers need to undergo many steps before the computation is successful. The algorithm has to solve multiple problems in different stages. This model considers a game of Sudoku, which can be easily solved using conventional digital computers using an analytically derived solution. However, quantum computers will take a longer time depending on how difficult the Sudoku puzzle is.

The third model of quantum computing is based on the idea of the mind map. This model focuses on the cognitive process of human beings and how it is associated with problem-solving. In this model, a human being goes through various stages before arriving at a solution. The first stage is a representation of the problem by a complex, high-dimensional graph called a "Mind Map". This graph is then turned into an "Action Map" by removing irrelevant information from it. The second stage is to obtain the probability of each action. The third stage is to select the best action to be taken.

A comparison of these models shows that they do not

describe all the steps required for successful quantum computer computations.

Another widely debated topic in these models is decoherence or interference between qubits. This model attempts to explain the operation of a quantum computer decoupling qubits using piecewise continuous decoherence functions, which combine many individual qubit operations into one long term average operation for simplicity.

11. DATA DETECTIVE: DATA DETECTIVE DATA MUNGING AND FINDING PATTERNS

Data detectives spend their days munging data; breaking down datasets into smaller, more manageable pieces that are easier to understand and analyze. Once the data comes together in one place, they can look for patterns like seasonal sales rates or correlations between two variables. Data detectives rely on their analytical skills to identify these patterns so they can help companies make decisions based on the results.

Data Munging (Data Wrangling)

A recent survey on the methods of munging and wrangling data has been presented by Chang et al. (2012). Their study proposed a framework for data munging, which comprises five steps: discover, clean, transform, enrich and validate. Most importantly, they also present an evaluation of available tools using a framework based on these steps.

Workflow of data wrangling for data scientists

Researchers have created tools that automate the process of wrangling data for data scientists. The workflows are based on the steps in munging and wrangling described above.

The following is an example of a simple workflow to automate the munging, cleaning, transforming and enriching steps.

Data wrangling is a tedious and time-consuming process. However, with the automation of the steps it takes only a few hours to mung and wrangle data for a project.

Munging is the process of combining data sets to create a single, more useful dataset. Oftentimes Data detectives will find multiple datasets on different websites, like the number of visitors to a particular site by month or the number of prospects who bought one product but not another. They must combine these sets into one dataset that can be analyzed in order to get accurate results. To do this they may have to set up criteria that only allows them to use certain pieces of data or enter values manually into a spreadsheet program. Munging data is a relatively simple process that has been used by Data detectives for a long time.

The Main 7 Steps In Data Wrangling Are As Follows:

1. Discovering: identify the source and form of data.

2. Structuring: identify the high-level schema of data.

3. Cleaning: improve the quality of data and integrate multiple datasets.

4. Enriching: add additional data to your datasets.

5. Validating: check if the data can be used and makes sense in a certain context (not necessary)

6. Understanding: explore, visualize and summarize data to find patterns and insights

7. Presenting: display and communicate insights in a meaningful way

Identifying Patterns

Once the munging is complete, Data detectives can begin looking for patterns. They first need to identify the variables they want to analyze and make sure they have all the values needed to make accurate conclusions. If there are multiple variables, they can use a spreadsheet to keep track of the relationships between them before beginning analysis. Data detectives review the data to identify any trends, seasonal changes or odd factors like an unusually high number of online visitors in one month. They will also consider the source, type and size of the data sets to help determine whether or not they can make any conclusions based on them. This process is much more complicated than it sounds; if even one piece of information is missing, the entire analysis may be useless.

Steps In Identifying Patterns

1. Identify what you want to analyze.

2. Decide on the variables of your choice, for example, demographics, sales data, etc.

3. Determine if all the values are available for use or if they are missing. If so, why might this be? If not, why not?

4. Make sure there are enough values to attempt an analysis without influencing the original data set so as not to contaminate it with invalid results.

5. Calculate correlations between each variable to identify relationships between them.

6. Draw conclusions from the findings of this analysis.

12. DATA DETECTIVE: CREATING COMPUTERISED MODELS TO EXTRACT THE DATA

Computer models are used in a wide variety of applications, from predicting the weather to figuring out how many words a person will type on a mobile device. Data detectives have been able to use computerized modelling to extract data from different sources and make sense of all the information related. In this chapter, we will be discussing these models as well as what they can do for you as an individual as well as organizations for the future.

Computer models are used in a wide variety of applications, from predicting the weather to figuring out how many words a person will type on a mobile device. Data detectives have been able to use computerized modelling to extract data from different sources and make sense of all the information related. In this chapter, we will be discussing these models as well as what they can do for you as an individual as well as organizations for the future.

Data represent facts that are gathered by scientists and stored in special places known as databases. A database could be made up of any material that is organized in such a way that it could be retrieved when needed. The material must contain information that is well structured to improve retrieval ability. This forms the basis of data modelling.

Data structures are the ways in which data are stored in different databases. A database can be categorized into 2 structures, firstly there is the Relational database that organizes the data into rows and columns. The other type of database is the document-based database that groups information into containers or documents. These two types of structure are common computerized models to help with retrieval, storage and retrieval of data.

The second requirement is to have a variety of access methods to allow users to retrieve information from specific databases. These methods are known as the query languages that allow you to retrieve information by making requests. Some of these interfaces that are used to retrieve data are DB, HTML, JSON, etc.

To build successful computerized models in the future, it is important to have the basics of data structure right. A database structure where you can easily retrieve data when required will help any organization to avoid problems in their operations.

DB is one of the main computerized models in use today that works on relational database structures for extracting data from different sources.

Steps To Building Complex Multi-Data Input Computerized Models

Step# 1: Identify the problem that you wish to solve

Step# 2: Work with the client to come up with a solution to the problem

Step# 3: Build a prototype of the solution together with verified data sources

Step# 4: Build an executable of your computerized model or Access to a database you created. You might want to look at DB database management software for this purpose.

Step# 5: Test and refine the model by seeing results and determining whether they meet
expectations

Example #1: A recent example where Data detectives were able to build computerized models has been in the insurance industry. An insurance company was able to reduce the time taken by their Data detective team to retrieve information from their databases using computerized models. The time taken to retrieve information went from 28 minutes to 2 minutes. This was done by building computerized models that allowed the Data detectives to easily retrieve information while solving the given problems.

Example #2: A recent example where Data detectives were able to build computerized models has been in the education sector. A large number of online courses are available on different websites which can be quite overwhelming for students who are looking for them. An online education company was able to use computerized models to create a website that would allow students to easily search for courses and put them on a list.

Example #3: A recent example where Data detectives were able to build computerized models has been in the medical sector. A company that provides medical records to other hospitals was able to build a computerized model that would allow them to search not only the information that they had but also retrieve information related as an important step in their processing of medical records.

13. DATA DETECTIVE: REMOVING CORRUPTED DATA

As a data detective, you need to know data is generated by the "N" number of sources from a user point of view or business point of view. Such as:

Internet Of Things Endpoints, Devices, Sensors, Biometric Monitors, Traditional Computing Infrastructure, Next-Gen Fog Mesh Edge Neural Capabilities, Advanced Artificial Intelligence Algorithms, EV – Electric Cars, Scooters Or Any Vehicles and Data Streaming From The Cloud…Etc

It is important to remove corrupted data or noise data from input. The process of data removal is much more than just filtering, there are many things to consider. It needs to be suitable for the level of data, the pattern to remove, the data itself, how you want it to be sent back etc. For example, if you are looking at an image that has distorted pixels then do you want that image or just a magnified version? This can be similar to what you would do with watermarking a piece of media content. Does the data removal need to remove image watermarks, text watermarks or just the noise?

Before data removal can take place, you will need to consider how the data is generated and which pattern you feel that best represents your needs. For example, if you are using one of the Ethernet technologies with a sensor attached, there are a range of patterns from which you can work with. The Ethernet standards have been designed for most Ethernet device types and Ethernet media types."

You may also approach this from a different direction. For example, what if you want to remove all noise from a file but the file is only 3 seconds long and 100MB in size, would you want to use a pattern such as FFT for this? Or perhaps one of the more complex patterns such as AWGN or Viterbi Compressed AWGN applied to this data?

The most important thing is that you align your performance goals with your business goals; otherwise, it will not be possible.

In the automotive industry, various designs have been found to be helpful in removing noise from sensors, facial recognition or even human interfaces. In facial recognition for instance, it is more important to get a clear picture of a face than it is for it to be low latency. But when you are looking at a sensor being used in a safety-critical system such as an emergency braking system, latency becomes the most important factor and low latency becomes a key business metric. This all depends on what your use-case is and who your business customers are.

In the following sections, we will discuss a number of common noise removal techniques and give an example or two.

Filtering is a commonly used method of removing noise from data. It can be used both in the time domain and spatial domain. In the spatial domain, we talk about using masks, grids and filters to remove noise. These can be either static or dynamic and can be symmetric or asymmetric, linear or non-linear, etc. In the time domain, we use recursive filters such as moving average, Kalman Filter etc. These are also either static or dynamic, linear or non-linear, etc.

Typically, when you are designing a filter system for this purpose, one of the key things to remember is that your filter system must preserve the integrity of your signal's data. You want to make sure that you are not corrupting your data with the noise removal systems that you place in place. If you do not, you will actually be decreasing the integrity of your data and cause yourself more problems than you originally intended to solve.

Before implementing any filtering or noise removal systems, it is critical that you validate your approach thoroughly. You need to make sure that the filter system is working in accordance with your expectations and does what you want it to do. Measurements of your application are crucial in this case. You will need to measure the level of noise being added to your signal, the fidelity of the data being generated, and ultimately your business metrics for evaluating whether or not you have achieved the goal that you set out to achieve.

Example #1:

If you want to remove some noise from your data you can perform some filtering on your data. There are several different approaches to filtering the data.

Filtering in the time domain: The simplest method of filtering would be to use a moving average filter or a digital signal processor (DSP). Most DSPs have one integrated within it. A good example of a moving average filter would be the simple moving average filter. This is also known as the Gaussian filter. This uses a linear function to decrease the output value by 1 each time it is calculated based on the input value. The output of this function tends to move toward zero, so it is called a Gaussian-like function.

If you are not familiar with how Gaussian filters work, think about what happens when you are looking at two people standing next to each other in line at a bank. If you look at the first person standing next to that person, the final signal that you want would be very close to your first input value. If you then take the output of this first-person and multiply it by the second input value, the output signal will be very close to your first input value. The reason why this works is that they are both standing next to each other, so their signal is not far from where it started. This is the same idea behind Gaussian filtering.

Filtering in the time domain can be used for removing high-frequency noise from your signal. If you simply look at the graph below, you will see that this graph shows a common band-limited impulse response filter "G". It has two poles at -6 dBm and +6 dBm, with all frequencies occurring at ±6 dB around them. The output of this filter has a 2 delta-sigma noise figure. The 1 dB time delay is selected such that the filter can suppress 10 dB of the noise at the −6 dBm and −12 dBm input levels. At −6 dBm and −12 dBm, 1 ms of filter time is required to pass all frequencies between −6 and +6 dBm (i.e. cutoff frequency). The filter roll-off rate can be selected from a -3 to 12 harmonically spaced octaves.

Example #2:

Let's assume that you want to remove some 1 Hz noise from the signal. This will come to a level of about 1 dB. The first step would be to create a graph of your data. Next, use the two-pole band-limited low pass filter "G" above to create an impulse response contour for this segment of your data. Finally, use the idealized gain curve shown below for this particular filter. The function is given below.

This will move the 1 Hz noise to levels less than 1 dB. It also moves the signal toward zero, so that is good!

The figure below shows the amplitude of the output of this filter after being smoothed with a 3 dB time-domain Butterworth low pass filter. We do this because it will make it easier to see how much of the noise has been removed from the signal. Our goal is to be able to see where the noise-free data begins. We are looking for the data points that are zero or below −132 dBm.

Example #3:

Let's extend the above example by adding some 1 kHz noise. This will come to a level of about 1 dB. The first step would be to create a graph of your data. Next, use the two-pole band-limited low pass filter "G" above to create an impulse response contour for this segment of your data. Finally, use the idealized gain curve shown below for this particular filter. The function is given below.

This moves the 1 Hz noise to levels less than 1 dB. It also moves the signal toward zero, so that is good!

The figure below shows the amplitude of the output of this filter after being smoothed with a 3 dB time-domain Butterworth low pass filter. We do this because it will make it easier to see how much of the noise has been removed from the signal. Our goal is to be able to see where the noise-free data begins. We are looking for the data points that are zero or below −132 dBm.

14. DATA DETECTIVE: PERFORM INITIAL ANALYSIS TO ASSESS THE QUALITY OF THE DATA

Do you have a pile of data but have no idea what to do with it?

When you have a set of data, or even when you just suspect that there might be some in your possession, the first thing an analyst should do is conduct an initial analysis to assess the quality of the data. This will help identify any obvious issues and improve your understanding of how to work with them going forward. It can also lead to identifying trends that weren't previously observable.

If the data appears to be of high quality, then you can move on to other tasks. However, if the data doesn't seem to be of good quality, then this initial analysis will provide you with vital information about how it should be processed moving forward.

An initial analysis will allow you to answer questions such as:

Data quality is an important aspect of your analysis. It has a significant effect on the value of your work and the quality required depends on your purpose for using the data.

The ability to clean your data so that you have a set that is of high quality is an essential part of data analysis. It allows you to carry out proper analysis and gain accurate results from your work. It also makes it easier to share this gathered knowledge with others, which means that your colleagues can understand what you have done and build on it with their own analysis.

You should always aim to work with data that is of the highest quality possible. However, steps can be taken to identify and resolve quality issues where necessary. If you are working with the data directly it is important to reduce any potential errors through recording methods, cleanly defined fields and effective organization (which allows you to easily find relevant information). When you are dealing with large volumes of data to analyze it is often better to sub-sample it or use domain-specific knowledge to narrow down your analysis parameters so that you can focus on relevant results.

When you are analyzing the data, it is important to identify any issues that arise. When your insights are built on low-quality data it is unlikely that these will provide an accurate reflection of the wider situation. It may even lead to incorrect conclusions being made. This can be detrimental to your work by leading you to make wrong decisions based on faulty information. Data quality issues can have a number of causes, which you may be able to identify through an initial analysis.

The Following Are A Few Examples Of Common Data Issues That Occur:

Visually examining a chart or graph is a good way to identify potential problems with the data. For example, if there appear to be gaps in the data then this could indicate that particular records have been removed from the dataset during processing. In this case, you should try to identify why this has occurred as it could lead to inaccurate interpretations of your conclusions.

You can also use statistical tests to help you identify if there is an issue with the data as a whole. This will be dependent on what you are analyzing and your purpose for using it. For example, if you are working with a spreadsheet full of customer data and want to identify if there is any missing information, such as first names or email addresses, then you can use a chi-square test. If you wanted to know if the responses given in a questionnaire were different then the two-sample t-test could be useful.

At the end of the analysis, you should summarize your findings and give it to someone else. When you give them your conclusions they will be able to provide their own analysis and insights, which can help to build on your work. This will potentially allow everyone involved to come to a more informed conclusion about what you have uncovered and how it can be interpreted going forward.

Steps To Finding The Quality Of The Data

Step #1: make a list of "questions to ask" and start by asking the key questions – what do we want to see? – and – what can we assume?

The first thing you need to do is make a list of the questions you want to be answered and start analyzing the data. It is important that you work with data that is as close to human readable as possible. This will help you to get the most accurate results.

The questions that are of relevance will vary depending on your purpose for working with the data. Some questions may be more important than others, but it is important not to make assumptions about what you should be looking for. It is also important not to ignore data that does not appear to offer certain or any relevant insights. This can lead to missing out on information that could have otherwise been beneficial.

Step #2: identify where the data is present – how can I compare across variables? How can I tell if there is missing information?

Once you have started your analysis, it is important to take a good look at the data itself. This will allow you to identify the different variables that are being used. It also means that you can ask yourself questions relating to how this data relates to other things. For example, how is the data related to socio-economic variables? How does it relate to other variables (such as age)?

It is important that you identify how the variables are related to each other. If you are analyzing survey data then it is often helpful to consolidate the different questions into categories, such as income, household expenditure and wealth. You can then investigate which categories seem to offer the best insight into your overall data set. For example, if you wanted to find out about poverty in Germany you could look at "income".

Once you have examined the data you will be able to identify if there are any potential issues with it. For example, if there is a change in the distribution of responses over time then this could be an indication that something has occurred during the survey process. If this occurred, for example during the coding process, then it may lead to inaccurate results being drawn from your analysis.

Step #3: analyze the data. What are the main patterns? Are there outliers or gaps in the data? Is it what I expected?

Once you have identified an issue with your data it is important to further investigate this. The issue may be minor, such as a logical inconsistency between two variables (such as income and expenditure), or it could go to the heart of your analysis. In some cases, the issue may only relate to a specific variable, but there may also be several inconsistencies throughout different variables.

If you find an issue, such as a gap in the data, then it is important to address it. It could be that the data was missing such as a natural event such as a flood or that the respondent did not respond to the survey entirely. In some situations, these issues may also lead to differing results which would need to be accounted for when drawing conclusions from your analysis.

Step #4: correct any issues in the data. It is important to fix any discrepancies that you find in your data. This will prevent inaccuracies from creeping in during the analysis stage and will ensure that your findings are as accurate as possible.

If you identify an issue with the data it is important to go through each variable and take action. For example, if you found a statistical error in the data then it is necessary to make an amendment to ensure that there are no further errors introduced during the analysis stage. This would ensure that your analyses and findings remain accurate and unbiased.

Step #5: identify whether you can use certain variables. Is there enough information in this data?

It is essential when working with data to make sure you have enough information in order to make valid conclusions from the analysis. If the dataset does not provide enough information for this, then it may be necessary to add extra variables to the dataset or add a further question in the questionnaire.

Step #6: identify whether there are any issues with the data or issues with how you are using it.

If you have come to a point in the analysis where it is clear that the data does not tell you what you need to know then it may be necessary to reconsider your approach or if required, look at other methods to obtain the information that you want. While this will not always be beneficial, it may be necessary in some situations.

Often, when working with large datasets, it is clear that the research questions were not sufficiently clear or that there were additional data needs. By addressing these issues at an early stage it will help to ensure that the resources are available to support your analysis.

Step #7: reanalyze the same information but using different methods. For example, you could use multiple regression or logistic regression.

At the analysis stage, it is important to use multiple methods of analysis. This will ensure that you can understand the patterns that are being produced by different methods. This also means that you can compare these results and identify any major discrepancies. This helps to improve your final conclusions by ensuring they are supported by independent evidence.

Step #8: interpret the results of your analysis/findings. Is there too much information? What does it all mean?

It is important to remember that just because you have conducted an analysis, it does not mean that you will immediately know the answers to your original questions. Analysis often produces large amounts of data and these can lead to complex patterns which are hard to interpret. However, if the analysis was conducted well, then this should be supported by clear evidence.

15. DATA DETECTIVE: DETERMINE THE MEANING OF THE DATA

Data detectives perform further analysis to determine the meaning of the data. It is important for analysts to know what kind of data they are analyzing so that they can interpret and draw usable information from it. Customers also need to know how and when their data is being analyzed and used so that they can understand how it affects them. Data analysis must be performed by an individual or a team that has been trained, has a high level of knowledge about the data they are analyzing and understands the processes involved with data analysis.

Data can be analyzed at different levels of detail, from very simple to highly complex. The types of analysis that can be performed on data include:

How To Determine The Meaning Of The Data

There is no hard and fast rule of how to determine the meaning of the data in order to draw out data analysis. It is important that analysts have a general understanding of the various terms or indicators that are being analyzed. The terms that are used to describe data are usually defined in the appropriate manual or guide. Analysts should also be able to recognize the terms that are being used, so they can understand how they are being analyzed.

There are many methods that people use to find meaning in data, some of the most popular include the following:

The Data detective is responsible for carrying out their analysis by following the appropriate processes. This includes using techniques such as charting, explaining results and making recommendations.

There are many different types of charts that can be used for data analysis.

The analyst should be responsible for how the data is displayed on the chart, ensuring that there is no misleading information included. For example, an analyst may choose to use a bar chart instead of a pie chart if there are more than three categories of information.

The analyst will also be responsible for the quality of their analysis. The quality of the analysis can be rated on several different levels including:

The analyst should provide an explanation of the results obtained from the data analysis, in addition to making recommendations about these results. They need to clearly explain not only what has been done but also why it has been done. To do this they need to use terms that are easy for their customers to understand while still maintaining a professional standard.

A Data detective is a person who performs data analysis to determine the meaning of the data. Data detectives need to have a general understanding of the terms used in their analysis, so they can recognize them when they are used. They also need to understand how data analysis works, in order to carry out their own analysis. Data detectives are usually found in an organization that processes or analyzes large quantities of data on a regular basis, or that requires its members to make decisions based on the information provided by the data.

The Data detective must also be able to work in a team, so they can communicate effectively and efficiently with other members of the team. They will also need to have a high level of knowledge about data analysis techniques, to make sure that they are performing their analysis correctly. It is important for them to be able to communicate effectively with others, especially the users who are receiving the results of their analysis. Analysts should be able to explain their analyses in an understandable way while maintaining a professional standard.

The IT department of an organization is responsible for delivering information to its customers. They must also be able to analyze large amounts of data in order to make decisions about the data.

16. DATA DETECTIVE: FINAL ANALYSIS TO PROVIDE ADDITIONAL DATA SCREENING

Data detectives perform further analysis to determine the meaning of the data. It is important for analysts to know what kind of data they are analyzing so that they can interpret and draw usable information from it. Customers also need to know how and when their data is being analyzed and used so that they can understand how it affects them. Data analysis must be performed by an individual or a team that has been trained, has a high level of knowledge about the data they are analyzing and understands the processes involved with data analysis.

Data can be analyzed at different levels of detail, from very simple to highly complex. The types of analysis that can be performed on data include:

How To Determine The Meaning Of The Data

There is no hard and fast rule of how to determine the meaning of the data in order to draw out data analysis. It is important that analysts have a general understanding of the various terms or indicators that are being analyzed. The terms that are used to describe data are usually defined in the appropriate manual or guide. Analysts should also be able to recognize the terms that are being used, so they can understand how they are being analyzed.

There are many methods that people use to find meaning in data, some of the most popular include the following:

The Data detective is responsible for carrying out their analysis by following the appropriate processes. This includes using techniques such as charting, explaining results and making recommendations.

There are many different types of charts that can be used for data analysis.

The analyst should be responsible for how the data is displayed on the chart, ensuring that there is no misleading information included. For example, an analyst may choose to use a bar chart instead of a pie chart if there are more than three categories of information.

The analyst will also be responsible for the quality of

their analysis. The quality of the analysis can be rated on several different levels including:

The analyst should provide an explanation of the results obtained from the data analysis, in addition to making recommendations about these results. They need to clearly explain not only what has been done but also why it has been done. To do this they need to use terms that are easy for their customers to understand while still maintaining a professional standard.

A Data detective is a person who performs data analysis to determine the meaning of the data. Data detectives need to have a general understanding of the terms used in their analysis, so they can recognize them when they are used. They also need to understand how data analysis works, in order to carry out their own analysis. Data detectives are usually found in an organization that processes or analyzes large quantities of data on a regular basis, or that requires its members to make decisions based on the information provided by the data.

The Data detective must also be able to work in a team, so they can communicate effectively and efficiently with other members of the team. They will also need to have a high level of knowledge about data analysis techniques, to make sure that they are performing their analysis correctly. It is important for them to be able to communicate effectively with others, especially the users who are receiving the results of their analysis. Analysts should be able to explain their analyses in an understandable way while maintaining a professional standard.

The IT department of an organization is responsible for

delivering information to its customers. They must also be able to analyze large amounts of data in order to make decisions about the data.

17. DATA DETECTIVE: REPRESENTING DATA TO MANAGEMENT

Data detectives preparing reports based on analysis and presenting to management.

Businesses are using data analytics in every sector of the world in order to make decisions. As a result, companies are starting to hire professional Data detectives, who use statistics in their portfolios of reports, in order to make business decisions for the company. For instance, they might examine market share trends or determine whether product development is best done for this type of consumer or that type. They might be asked to make predictions on earnings or sales as well as provide advice for how to improve financial results. They might also be asked to forecast weather on a long-term basis and analyze potential revenue for a company.

Before deciding whether data analysis is required for production, businesses first need to determine if the task can be done by hand. A business may feel that it is possible to correctly forecast sales and customer needs by simply looking at historical data, but there are significant risks involved in this approach. For example, companies may have problems determining patterns or trends within historical data.

One common issue involved is an overreliance on historical data, which represents the past rather than the present. The past has little resemblance to the future for many companies, and it is often impossible to determine how situations will progress by looking at historical results. A second issue that might arise is that of failing to include recent changes in the data. For instance, certain factors like market saturation or new technology may alter how a business can best respond to its customers. Therefore, if a company is unable to forecast sales and other results through data analysis, it may need to hire a professional who can do the job.

Once the decision has been made to hire a professional Data detective, there are several factors involved in managing this position. For example, a business should have a set of objectives for this position before searching for candidates. If the company is looking for someone who will evaluate market trends, it must be clear about what types of trends should be tracked and how trends will be used in decision making. Once this is clear, the company can then begin to search for potential candidates.

The first stop is likely to be an online job chaptering site, where companies can list their openings and look through resumes submitted by candidates. A company may also submit its requirements for this position to employment agencies that specialize in finding candidates with the right skills for specific positions. This includes not only basic qualifications like education, experience, and professional certifications but also certain personality traits that will help the candidate succeed.

While some companies will want workaholic candidates, others are looking for low-key coworkers who are willing to follow the process without being too demanding. If a company is able to find qualified candidates with the right skill set, it may choose to use an in-house Data detective, who will be expected to report directly to the business' CEO or another executive leadership team.

When managing this position, a business should have a clear understanding of what data analysis entails. For example, a business should be able to define different types of reports that a Data detective might produce as well as how these reports will be used. A company also needs to understand if this position will need to do research work in addition to producing reports and if there are any rules for interacting with other departments. For example, Data detectives may need to interact with sales or the marketing department on the project at hand.

A company must also be sure it understands the importance of clearly specifying what type of data is needed. For instance, if a company asks for data that doesn't exist, the Data detective may have to request more information or come up with an alternative way to get the information. A business should also think about how this position might be used in the future, and therefore build in opportunities for promotion, training, or new responsibilities for this position.

How To Present Data To Management

For a Data detective to provide a report to management it is important that the Q&A session is structured, as well as concise and to the point. The report should start at the beginning with a clear statement of the problem that has been faced and a definition of terms. You will then go into a brief presentation of your findings. Explain your process and how you arrived at your results. You must be very strong on what you found and focused on only those facts which support your conclusions. When conveying your findings, it is important that you are not over-dramatic. The Data detective should frame the report so it gives management an overview of the situation and answer any questions they might have.

There should be no personal opinions or emotional statements inserted into the report. It is important to understand management has already made the decision about which presentation styles work for them, so use their preferred style to present your data. One important rule about presenting data to management is that the report should be factual and objective, not just opinionated.

Data analysis is widely used in planning, forecasting, and decision support for many industries. The activities of data analysis help businesses to identify potential areas for improvement and to better understand their markets. Data analysis is also used to gather insights that will give businesses valuable information on the performance of their business operations, improve decision-making methods, adjust operations or policy changes, or act in response to trends identified.

18. DATA DETECTIVE BIG DATA AND AI/ML

A new breed of a Data detective is beginning to emerge. With the advent of big data and more specifically machine learning, the introduction of artificial intelligence, and analytics technology, it has never been easier for aspiring Data detectives to get into this field. Big Data is used in virtually every industry today to help determine why some companies are more successful than others. For example, Netflix's success over the years has been attributed solely to its ability to not only analyze customer feedback but also create personalized content based on that feedback. The company uses artificial intelligence to create its best shows and even employs more than 100 Data detectives.

A new breed of a Data detective is emerging. With the advent of big data and more specifically machine learning, the introduction of artificial intelligence, and analytics technology, it has never been easier for aspiring Data detectives to get into this field. Big Data is used in virtually every industry today to help determine why some companies are more successful than others. For example, Netflix's success over the years has been attributed solely to its ability to not only analyze customer feedback but also create personalized content based on that feedback. The company uses artificial intelligence to create its best shows and even employs more than 100 Data detectives.

Big Data is used in virtually every industry today to help determine why some companies are more successful than others. For example, Netflix's success over the years has been attributed solely to its ability to not only analyze customer feedback but also create personalized content based on that feedback. The company uses artificial intelligence to create its best shows and even employs more than 100 Data detectives.

The Data Detective's New Role

Over the past few years, the role of Data detective has become much more prominent. The demand for Data detectives is now so great that it seems like there are more people trying to enter the field than there are jobs available. This is due to the fact that big data is becoming a bigger part of our modern-day society, leaving many organizations scrambling to find skilled workers who can extract meaning from all this data. According to the Bureau of Labor Statistics, the number of jobs for Data detectives is expected to increase by 29 percent within the next decade. This is higher than the overall growth rate, which is expected to be about 14 percent. There are currently more than 300,000 people employed in this field. Demand for competent Data detectives is only going to continue growing.

The Importance Of Data Analysis

Data analysis has become one of the most important aspects of business today. This process is used to find trends and patterns within the large amounts of data that businesses and other organizations collect. For example, data analysis can be used to determine which advertisements are most popular or to determine what kind of music is played in a store. This makes analyzing big data such a highly sought-after skill because it can help companies make smarter business decisions which in turn leads to increased profits.

Data analysis has become one of the most important aspects of business today. This process is used to find trends and patterns within the large amounts of data that businesses and other organizations collect. For example, data analysis can be used to determine which advertisements are most popular or to determine what kind of music is played in a store. This makes analyzing big data such a highly sought-after skill because it can help companies make smarter business decisions which in turn leads to increased profits.

Data analysis has become one of the most important aspects of business today. This process is used to find trends and patterns within the large amounts of data that businesses and other organizations collect. For example, data analysis can be used to determine which advertisements are most popular or to determine what kind of music is played in a store. This makes analyzing big data such a highly sought-after skill because it can help companies make smarter business decisions which in turn leads to increased profits.

The Data detective's Needs

Given the increased demand for Data detectives, one of the biggest challenges that aspiring Data detectives face is finding ways to learn the necessary skills. Data analysis requires a lot of education and training. While there are programs available to help aspiring candidates become trained Data detectives, most candidates are not able to enroll in these programs due to strict enrollment criteria. This makes it difficult for candidates to compete with others who already have experience because employers understand that they are entering a highly competitive field.

Given the increased demand for Data detectives, one of the biggest challenges that aspiring Data detectives face is finding ways to learn the necessary skills. Data analysis requires a lot of education and training. While there are programs available to help aspiring candidates become trained Data detectives, most candidates are not able to enroll in these programs due to strict enrollment criteria. This makes it difficult for candidates to compete with others who already have experience because employers understand that they are entering a highly competitive field.

Given the increased demand for Data detectives, one of the biggest challenges that aspiring Data detectives face is finding ways to learn the necessary skills. Data analysis requires a lot of education and training. While there are programs available to help aspiring candidates become trained Data detectives, most candidates are not able to enroll in these programs due to strict enrollment criteria. This makes it difficult for candidates to compete with others who already have experience because employers understand that they are entering a highly competitive field.

Given the increased demand for Data detectives, one of the biggest challenges that aspiring Data detectives face is finding ways to learn the necessary skills. Data analysis requires a lot of education and training. While there are programs available to help aspiring candidates become trained Data detectives, most candidates are not able to enroll in these programs due to strict enrollment criteria. This makes it difficult for candidates to compete with others who already have experience because employers understand that they are entering a highly competitive field.

The Solution. Big data is in high demand today, and one of the fastest ways to analyze it is through cloud computing. Cloud computing can dramatically speed up the amount of time that it takes for Data detectives to analyze large amounts of information, which means that organizations are able to get faster results. It also offers increased security, allowing companies to store sensitive customer information online without worry. Cloud data storage also allows organizations to take advantage of multiple server locations which makes it easier to run their businesses around the world.

Big data is in high demand today, and one of the fastest ways to analyze it is through cloud computing. Cloud computing can dramatically speed up the amount of time that it takes for Data detectives to analyze large amounts of information, which means that organizations are able to get faster results. It also offers increased security, allowing companies to store sensitive customer information online without worry. Cloud data storage also allows organizations to take advantage of multiple server locations which makes it easier to run their businesses around the world.

FOLLOW ALONG THE JOURNEY

This book showcases the future data-driven job "Data Detective". The author, who is himself a data detective, has gone on to share the expertise that comes with this job. The book showcases how one can be a "data detective". It also stresses some important skills for this job.

The book emphasizes the importance of different skills

while looking at data. For example, it highlights the role of domain expertise in making judgements about data. Other important skills include an ability to understand the basics of statistics and physics (different types of sensors).

The book is mainly focused on the job title "Data Detective". The author of the book himself has worked as a data detective and has gone on to share his expertise in the field. In the book, the author gives a brief explanation of how one can become a data detective or enhance their skills in this field. The book also talks about the skills required if someone wants to be a data detective.

The author stresses some important themes such as representing data to management, overcoming challenges with sensor aggregation etc.. The author has used his own experiences to help the reader understand the concepts.

Before I finish reading this book! Let us make some notes

Why do I need to become a Data Detective?

Do I have all the skills to become an Data Detective?

_____

_____

_____

_____

How does Data Detective work In the Agile Era?

_____

_____

_____

_____

What are the recent development about Quantum
Computing area

_____

_____

_____

_____

What are the main AI/ML, BIG DATA Skills you need for
this job?

_____

_____

_____

_____

In future what are the different "N" numbers of sources we
will collect the data?

_____

How to present data to management?

Steps in Removing Corrupted Data?

How to perform initial analysis to assess the quality of the data?

_____

_____

_____

_____

_____

_____

_____

_____

_____

_____

_____

How final analysis to provide additional data screening
Final analysis to provide additional data screening?

_____

_____

_____

_____

_____

_____

_____

_____

_____

_____

_____

_____

My top 11 take-away from this book

ABOUT THE AUTHOR

Padmaraj Nidagundi, the author of many books, works as an engineer, among other works, lives in Latvia, Riga, with his wife, Alina, and their one child. In this book, the author's goal is to bring the best technical life experiences lessons.

Printed in Great Britain
by Amazon

38868608R00056